# Har

## *Is Not the*

# Same Thing

# *as* Bad

## STUDY GUIDE

# Abbie Halberstadt

Illustrations by Lindsay Long

**HARVEST HOUSE PUBLISHERS**
EUGENE. OREGON

Cover design by Faceout Studio, Molly von Borstel
Cover photo © natrot / Shutterstock; cover illustrations © Celia Baker
Interior design by Janelle Coury
Interior Illustrations by Lindsay Long

For bulk, special sales, or ministry purchases, please call 1-800-547-8979.
Email: CustomerService@hhpbooks.com

**Hard Is Not the Same Thing as Bad Study Guide**

Copyright © 2024 by Abbie Halberstadt
Published by Harvest House Publishers
Eugene, Oregon 97408
www.harvesthousepublishers.com

ISBN 978-0-7369-9101-8 (pbk)

**Printed in the United States of America**

24 25 26 27 28 29 30 31 32 / KP / 10 9 8 7 6 5 4 3 2 1

# Contents

# Introduction

Have you ever thought, "I really don't like this _____ (circumstance, season, problem, pain). I'd just like to skip it, please"? Or maybe a less polite version? Maybe you've slammed your palm against the wall, screamed into your pillow, cursed into the silence of your car? Even if none of these exact scenarios ring a bell, the fact remains that, if you're breathing, you've experienced hard things. Jesus literally promised us we would encounter "trouble" in this world (John 16:33 NIV). It's the human condition. Not only that, but He declares this fact within the context of just having warned His disciples of the coming of their darkest days (Christ's crucifixion). The weird part? He doesn't tell them so they will freak out or panic. No, He gives them a glimpse into a difficult future so that they "may have peace." If that sounds like a paradox of the highest order, I agree. It sure can seem that way. But as uncomfortably as it sits in our chests sometimes, there *is* a certain peace to be found in expecting hard things. When we know everything won't always be smooth paths and rose gardens but that, even so, Jesus has "overcome the world," we are empowered to face hardship with the knowledge that we stumble along bumpy paths with Christ ever by our side.

*Hard Is Not the Same Thing as Bad* is your invitation, not to cheer every time something "goes wrong" but to face each and every hard thing with the peace and confidence that Jesus has borne our sorrow, even to the point of death on a cross. I wrote this for moms, but I believe the biblical principles permeating each chapter are for every believer in Christ who desires to move beyond an attitude of escaping hardship into a mindset of overcoming in Christ's strength.

In this study guide, you'll find practical action steps, thought-provoking questions, a helpful chart breaking down the dichotomy of a worldly mindset about hard things versus a biblical one, space to record your thoughts, and even a format that will enable you to transform this from a time of personal reflection into a group study if you feel so led. I've also provided a QR code to allow access to accompanying video content from me for each chapter. This is the ideal companion to the book and study guide to help you take these truths to heart.

**Video Link**

I'll be the first to admit I don't like most hard things I encounter any more than the next girl. But I'll also be the first to proclaim my gratitude that the Lord has seen fit to carry me through the trials He's entrusted to me because I *know* I'm changed for the better by them.

# A Tiny
# Perspective Shift

## REAPING THE BENEFITS OF LOOKING
## AT HARD A WHOLE NEW WAY

The first chapter explores the perspective shift that takes place when we flip our knee-jerk tendency to view hard things as negative—as something from which to run—and replace it with a willingness to consider that the hardship itself might be a tool the Lord is using to shape us. Our culture constantly encourages us to escape or slough off experiences or people that don't "serve us," which can make switching into a mindset of viewing trials as potential sandpaper to smooth out our rough edges and to reveal our need for Christ feel downright jarring. But, as I share through personal experiences, when we turn toward Jesus instead of toward entertainment or numbness or anger, the maturity we gain is an incredible gift from God. The growth is worth the grit!

 **The Narrative**

Read the examples in your book of a worldly response to hard versus a biblical response to hard. Take some time to pray about the areas in which you might be embracing a worldly "mindset of hard," and record them here. Then reflect on what those same issues might look like through a Christian perspective of biblical truth.

| THE WORLD'S RESPONSE TO HARD | A CHRISTIAN RESPONSE TO HARD |
| --- | --- |
| | |
| | |
| | |

## ~~~∗∗∗ Action Steps ∗∗∗~~~

Write out, memorize, and meditate on 2 Timothy 4:7: "I have fought the good fight, I have finished the race, I have kept the faith." One helpful way to memorize Scripture is to start by writing it down.

---

---

---

---

---

---

---

Write five sticky notes with "hard ≠ bad" on them and post them in high-traffic areas of your home as reminders of this tiny perspective shift. How has seeing this message made a difference for you?

---

---

---

---

---

---

---

---

---

I have
fought
the good
fight,
I have
finished
the
race,
I have
kept
the faith.

2 TIMOTHY 4:7

Pray about one friend who could help hold you accountable in changing the way you view the hard things in motherhood. Reach out when the Lord brings someone to mind. Who will you reach out to?

## Reflection Questions

Do I view hard primarily as bad? (Explain.)

If so, am I getting this view from worldly culture or the Bible?

_____

_____

_____

_____

_____

What is something hard in motherhood right now that the Lord is also using for good? And how?

_____

_____

_____

_____

_____

_____

_____

_____

_____

_____

_____

_____

## Group Discussion Questions

What is your initial response to the phrase "hard is not the same thing as bad"?

What is one practical thing (not mentioned in the book) that would help this perspective shift sink in for you?

**Video Link**

Can you describe a time in your motherhood journey when the Lord has clearly met you in and carried you through your hardship?

_____

_____

_____

_____

_____

_____

_____

_____

_____

Apart from Christ, we are all going to struggle to view hard things with anything but resentment. How does that realization change the way you see a trial you've experienced (or are currently experiencing)?

_____

_____

_____

_____

_____

_____

_____

_____

_____

How can hardship help us conform to the image of Christ?

_____

_____

_____

_____

_____

_____

_____

_____

_____

_____

_____

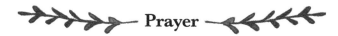 **Prayer**

*Lord, thank You that Jesus "for the joy that was set before him endured
the cross, despising the shame" (Hebrews 12:2), and, in the process, set
the ultimate example of hard not being the same thing as bad. Help
us to shift our mindsets from negativity to joy in You by Your strength.*

# Hard Things Are Not Always Suffering

## KEEPING PERSPECTIVE IN THE MIDST OF THE STRUGGLE

This chapter encourages us to examine our hard circumstances with clear eyes and honesty. Are we maximizing our struggles for attention or exaggerating them at times? Or conversely, are we so determined to downplay the hard that we minimize or invalidate our need for help and end up refusing opportunities for comfort (from God and others)? The Bible goes to neither extreme, instead exhorting us to mourn with those who mourn while still pressing into the "enoughness" of Christ's strength. We are not motherhood martyrs, but neither are we hardship deniers. It's truly possible to honor the hard in motherhood while not placing it on a pedestal as the ultimate suffering.

## The Narrative

Read the examples in your book of a worldly response to hard versus a biblical response to hard. Take some time to pray about the areas in which you might be embracing a worldly "mindset of hard," and record them here. Then reflect on what those same issues might look like through a Christian perspective of biblical truth.

| THE WORLD'S RESPONSE TO HARD | A CHRISTIAN RESPONSE TO HARD |
| --- | --- |
| | |
| | |
| | |

## ⊱⊱⊱ Action Steps ⊰⊰⊰

Write out, memorize, and meditate on 2 Corinthians 4:16: "So we do not lose heart. Though our outer self is wasting away, our inner self is being renewed day by day."

_____

_____

_____

_____

_____

_____

_____

_____

_____

_____

Write down two things you have viewed as suffering that are actually just God-given challenges.

1. _____

_____

_____

2. _____

_____

_____

Ask your accountability partner from the last chapter to pray for you to view these two struggles rightly as you mother this week. Record here the prayer requests she has for you.

_____

_____

_____

_____

_____

_____

_____

_____

## Reflection Questions

Why (biblically) does God allow us to experience hard things?

_____

_____

_____

_____

_____

_____

_____

How does viewing hard things as the challenges they are (instead of viewing them as suffering) materially affect the way I treat my children?

_____

_____

_____

_____

_____

_____

_____

What are two specific ways I can grow in Christlikeness through the challenges I'm experiencing?

1. _____

_____

_____

_____

2. _____

_____

_____

_____

**Group Discussion Questions**

Up to this point, what has been your definition of "hard" in motherhood?

_____

_____

_____

_____

_____

_____

_____

What have you heard, seen, or read lately that encourages you to view yourself as a victim or martyr of motherhood?

_____

_____

_____

_____

_____

**Video Link**

_____

_____

_____

Can you think of a time in your life when your own mother (or another adult or "mother figure") implied that caring for you was a form of suffering? If so, how did that make you feel?

_____

_____

_____

_____

_____

_____

_____

What are some "words of life" you can speak over your family this week?

_____

_____

_____

_____

_____

_____

_____

_____

_____

What is one practical way you can intentionally shift your mindset from "have to" to "get to" this week?

_____

_____

_____

_____

_____

_____

_____

_____

_____

_____

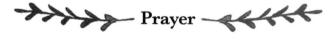

**Prayer**

*Lord, thank You that we really can do "all things through Christ who strengthens [us]" (Philippians 4:13 NKJV)—including finding contentment in hard circumstances. Grant us eyes to see the opportunities for sanctification and growth tucked inside each new mothering challenge we encounter.*

# The Problem
# with Easy

## GROWTH REQUIRES
## STRUGGLE

This chapter faces head-on the reality that not one of us is surprised when we learn that an Olympic athlete's training regimen is grueling and relentless. That's how they achieve excellence, right? And yet, when it comes to investing in, training, loving, and discipling an eternal soul, we can quickly succumb to the expectation of ease...and to resentment if it doesn't come. It's not about only wishing for hard. After all, the Lord is gracious to give us the good gift of easy seasons too. It's about recognizing that struggle brings growth. And without engaging in that struggle, we often stay stuck.

# The Narrative

Read the examples in your book of a worldly response to hard versus a biblical response to hard. Take some time to pray about the areas in which you might be embracing a worldly "mindset of hard," and record them here. Then reflect on what those same issues might look like through a Christian perspective of biblical truth.

| THE WORLD'S RESPONSE TO HARD | A CHRISTIAN RESPONSE TO HARD |
| --- | --- |
| | |
| | |
| | |

## ◄►►► Action Steps ◄◄◄

Write out, memorize and meditate on Romans 12:1-2: "I appeal to you therefore, brothers, by the mercies of God, to present your bodies as a living sacrifice, holy and acceptable to God, which is your spiritual worship. Do not be conformed to this world, but be transformed by the renewal of your mind, that by testing you may discern what is the will of God, what is good and acceptable and perfect."

Identify one thing you do *because* it's easier (not better), and pray about a game plan to go about it in a more God-honoring way.

Text your accountability partner at least once this week to let her know your plan and let her know you're praying for her (and then *actually* pray for her!). What are you praying for?

_____

_____

_____

_____

_____

_____

_____

_____

## Reflection Questions

Why, when Scripture makes it so clear that hard things will be part of this earthly life (John 16:33), do I sometimes avoid them at all costs?

_____

_____

_____

_____

_____

_____

COUNT IT ALL JOY... WHEN YOU MEET TRIALS OF VARIOUS KINDS.

JAMES 1:2

What is one motherhood goal I can set for myself that would require me to practically implement the concept "Growth requires struggle"?

_____

_____

_____

_____

_____

_____

What are two easy "sweet spot" aspects of motherhood right now that I can thank God for?

1. _____

_____

2. _____

_____

## Group Discussion Questions

What is one thing you're better at *as a result* of walking through a motherhood struggle?

_____

_____

_____

_____

_____

Who are some "heroes of hard" that come to mind as examples of persevering (and reaping the fruit as a result)?

What advice would you give your younger self now that you've walked some of the hard roads of motherhood?

**Video Link**

Why are we okay with other professions doggedly pursuing excellence while still wanting motherhood to be easy (or at least easier)?

---

What is one area in which the Lord is asking you to lean into the growth process of refining motherhood?

---

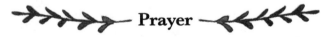 **Prayer**

*Lord, You know our tendency toward escapism, and yet You
never escape from us. Thank You that we were "called to
freedom" (Galatians 5:13), not as an occasion for indulging our
flesh but for serving one another in love. Give us fresh eyes to
see the incredible benefit of persevering through hard things.*

# The Hard (but Better) Road of Motherhood

## IT WON'T LOOK THE SAME FOR ALL OF US

This chapter examines our tendency to compare and contrast our own hard. We often strive for commonality of suffering—an assurance that we have all booked a ticket on the same struggle bus *and* that we've all gotten the same seat. But that's almost never the case. Even when we can relate to a fellow mama's struggle, our seasons might not jibe perfectly, nor will the severity of her plight be the same as ours. Secular culture encourages us to look for "relatability." But what if we don't find it, and yet the Lord still requires us to stay the course, even when no one else understands or relates? I share personal examples of women in my own life who inspire me with their particular brands of "hard" and their particular brands of biblical courage as they face their struggles head-on. Be encouraged that the Lord has called you to your specific circumstances for just such a time as this *on purpose.*

 **The Narrative**

Read the examples in your book of a worldly response to hard versus a biblical response to hard. Take some time to pray about the areas in which you might be embracing a worldly "mindset of hard," and record them here. Then reflect on what those same issues might look like through a Christian perspective of biblical truth.

| THE WORLD'S RESPONSE TO HARD | A CHRISTIAN RESPONSE TO HARD |
| --- | --- |
| | |
| | |
| | |

## ~~~ Action Steps ~~~

Write out, memorize, and meditate on Philippians 1:21: "For to me to live is Christ, and to die is gain."

Write down one area in which the Lord is calling you to choose the "hard but better" road in motherhood. (Your family's health? Personal time with the Lord? Schooling choices?)

Touch base with your accountability partner and commit to praying over these areas of conviction this week. Record here the prayer requests she has for you.

_____

_____

_____

_____

_____

_____

_____

## Reflection Questions

How do I respond when friends, family, or strangers mock me for pursuing a path of "unnecessary hardship" (in their eyes)?

_____

_____

_____

_____

_____

_____

_____

_____

_____

_____

Is my response biblical? Why or why not?

In what ways am I *privileged* to endure hardship for the sake of Christ and my family's growth?

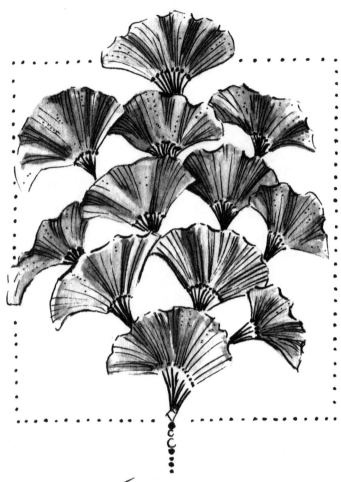

To live is
Christ,
and
to die is gain.

PHILIPPIANS 1:21

## Group Discussion Questions

What is an area of hard in motherhood you *know* the Lord wants you to persevere in right now?

Does anyone you know share the same struggle? Whether the answer is yes or no, how does that affect your attitude toward your circumstances?

**Video Link**

Does approval (or criticism) affect your desire to "stay the course"?

_____

_____

_____

_____

_____

_____

_____

Do you ever find yourself racking up "points" in a "crisis contest" with your peers (even if only in your head)? Is this biblical?

_____

_____

_____

_____

_____

_____

_____

_____

_____

_____

Who is one person you can pray for or reach out to who might need encouragement to keep choosing the hard (but better) road in motherhood?

_____

_____

_____

_____

_____

_____

_____

_____

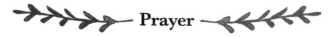 **Prayer**

*Lord, we know that You chose the hard road of the cross for our sakes, and yet we so often want to coast in Your grace, rather than pressing "on toward the goal for the prize of the upward call of God in Christ Jesus" (Philippians 3:14). Help us to freely embrace Your example of following the hard, but better, road in motherhood.*

# Fear Is a Liar

## WE CAN DO MORE HARD THINGS
## THAN WE THINK WE CAN

This chapter tackles our desire to hide from hard when we're afraid. If you had told my sixteen-year-old self I would be a mother of ten one day, I'm sure I would have panicked at least a little. "*Ten* children? But I have almost no experience with one child. I *can't* do that. I'm scared." Thankfully, the Lord is faithful to give us what we need when we need it (sometimes, not a moment sooner). But if the frequent messages about how fearful so many mamas are to have another child, adopt, start a business, home-school, write a book, preach the gospel, parent teens (and on and on) are any indication, "scared spitless" is a really easy place to live. Which is why the Bible tells us some version of "do not fear" 365 times. The Lord is not surprised by our fear. He is faithful to stay right by our sides through it. But He doesn't let us off the hook of taking action, even when we'd rather stay frozen.

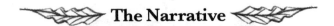 **The Narrative**

Read the examples in your book of a worldly response to hard versus a biblical response to hard. Take some time to pray about the areas in which you might be embracing a worldly "mindset of hard," and record them here. Then reflect on what those same issues might look like through a Christian perspective of biblical truth.

| THE WORLD'S RESPONSE TO HARD | A CHRISTIAN RESPONSE TO HARD |
|---|---|
| | |
| | |
| | |

## Action Steps

Write out, memorize, and meditate on Hebrews 11:1-3: "Faith is the assurance of things hoped for, the conviction of things not seen. For by it the people of old received their commendation. By faith we understand that the universe was created by the word of God, so that what is seen was not made out of things that are visible."

<br>
<br>
<br>
<br>

Identify and write down two motherhood areas that cause you consistent worry.

1. _____

2. _____

Choose one area to pray for specifically once a day this week with an attitude of "Thy will be done, Lord."

<br>
<br>
<br>
<br>

  **Reflection Questions**

What has the Lord called you to that you're afraid of right now?

In obeying Him, what is the worst thing that could happen? What's the best?

# BE STRONG AND COURAGEOUS.

JOSHUA 1:9

How has God shown Himself faithful in the past during challenging times?

_____

_____

_____

_____

_____

_____

_____

## Group Discussion Questions

What is something the Lord required you to "do scared" in the past? How did it turn out?

_____

_____

_____

_____

_____

_____

_____

_____

Satan is the father of lies. What is one lie he's trying to convince you of right now?

_____

_____

_____

_____

_____

_____

_____

_____

If your child were to come to you too scared to move forward with something, how would you encourage them?

_____

_____

_____

_____

_____

_____

_____

_____

_____

**Video Link**

How can we apply this encouragement to our own lives?

-------------------------------------------------------------

-------------------------------------------------------------

-------------------------------------------------------------

-------------------------------------------------------------

-------------------------------------------------------------

-------------------------------------------------------------

Is there anything impossible for God? If the answer is no, what does that mean for us?

-------------------------------------------------------------

-------------------------------------------------------------

-------------------------------------------------------------

-------------------------------------------------------------

-------------------------------------------------------------

-------------------------------------------------------------

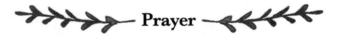 **Prayer**

*Lord, You have not given us a spirit of fear but of "power and love and self-control" (2 Timothy 1:7). Thank You for never leaving us or forsaking us. May we continue to recognize Your faithfulness to us as we take tiny steps of faith to obey You in the little things, the hard things, and the scary things.*

# Gluttons for Punishment

## WHEN THE HARD IS ACTUALLY OUR FAULT

This chapter asks us to be honest about those times we're our own worst enemies. Maybe it's a bad habit we've been "too tired" to tackle for ten years. Maybe we're starting to see the habit trickle down into our kids' attitudes and actions, and we realize just how big the toll will be if we don't address it in ourselves first. Whatever the issue, we can often be the architects of our most frustrating circumstances. The good news is that the truth of Scripture has the ability to help us be honest about the areas in which we could improve. But the Word also offers so much grace for our imperfections and struggles. What a kind and gracious God who calls us onward and upward while filling us with His Holy Spirit every step of the way.

# The Narrative

Read the examples in your book of a worldly response to hard versus a biblical response to hard. Take some time to pray about the areas in which you might be embracing a worldly "mindset of hard," and record them here. Then reflect on what those same issues might look like through a Christian perspective of biblical truth.

| THE WORLD'S RESPONSE TO HARD | A CHRISTIAN RESPONSE TO HARD |
| --- | --- |
|  |  |
|  |  |
|  |  |

## ⤳⤳ Action Steps ⤝⤝

Write out, memorize, and meditate on Proverbs 19:20-21: "Listen to advice and accept instruction, that you may gain wisdom in the future. Many are the plans in the mind of man, but it is the purpose of the LORD that will stand."

_____

_____

_____

_____

_____

Identify two ways in which you might be the architect of your own misery (hard situations, suffering, discomfort).

1. _____

_____

2. _____

_____

Write down three things (setting timers, going to bed earlier, memorizing verses) that could help you begin to break away from those unhelpful habits. Let your accountability partner know about your plans.

1. _____

_____

2. _____

_____

3. _____

_____

HE GIVES TO HIS BELOVED SLEEP.

PSALM 127:2

**Reflection Questions**

Why do we sometimes continue in unwise practices even though they cause us so many problems?

What does the Bible have to say about wise decision-making? (You can do internet searches like "verses about wisdom," "time management," or "good choices" for a quick dive into this topic.)

Who benefits the most when we shift to a mindset of overcomer in Christ from one of victimhood to our own bad choices?

_____

_____

_____

_____

_____

_____

## Group Discussion Questions

What is one "shoot yourself in the foot" area you've been avoiding?

_____

_____

_____

_____

_____

_____

_____

_____

_____

What are two practical ways you could start addressing the issue *today*?

When you notice things in your children that frustrate you, do you sometimes recognize the same tendency in your own life?

**Video Link**

In what ways does God offer grace to us when we "insist" on making our own lives hard?

_____

_____

_____

_____

_____

_____

_____

_____

Are we receptive to advice and admonishment from those close to us when they notice areas of self-destruction? Why or why not?

_____

_____

_____

_____

_____

_____

_____

_____

_____

_____

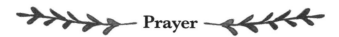 **Prayer**

*Jesus, You are perfect and sinless, and yet You chose to "seek not my own will but the will of him who sent me" (John 5:30). Convict our hearts to emulate Your example instead of clinging to bad habits (simply because they are comfortable) that are harming the peace of our homes.*

 If you need a reset in your ability to use kind speech and calm tones, consider a thirty-day commitment to the Gentleness Challenge. I detail this at length in *M Is for Mama*, and in my step-by-step e-book, available at misformama.net/downloads/the-gentleness-challenge.

# When We Can't Escape the Hard

## LOOKING FOR GOD'S GOODNESS WHEN WE FEEL STUCK

This chapter examines the situations in our lives for which there is no "solution" and from which there is no reasonable escape. Maybe, like me, you have a difficult relationship with a parent or other family member whom the Lord has given you to love. Maybe it's something entirely different. We've already talked about how varied our different "hards" can be. But the fact remains that each of us will, at some point in our lives, very likely encounter a trial for which the only way is through (and through and through). The answer to our difficulty may not even present itself in this lifetime. The good news is, dealing with the pain and constancy of an inescapable hard requires us to lean all the more on the kindness of Jesus. And He always has enough strength to support our weight.

# The Narrative

Read the examples in your book of a worldly response to hard versus a biblical response to hard. Take some time to pray about the areas in which you might be embracing a worldly "mindset of hard," and record them here. Then reflect on what those same issues might look like through a Christian perspective of biblical truth.

| THE WORLD'S RESPONSE TO HARD | A CHRISTIAN RESPONSE TO HARD |
|---|---|
| | |
| | |
| | |

## ⋙⋙ Action Steps ⋘⋘

Write out, memorize, and meditate on Psalm 27:13 (NIV): "I remain confident of this: I will see the goodness of the LORD in the land of the living."

_____

_____

_____

_____

_____

_____

_____

If a particular "inescapable hard" came to mind as you read this chapter, record it here. Take some time to ask the Lord to show you ways this situation has been a force for good in your life (even if it's just in demonstrating your need for Jesus).

_____

_____

_____

_____

_____

_____

_____

_____

_____

Ask the Lord to remind you of someone who might need encouragement that their inescapable hard is not hopeless and that they will still see the goodness of the Lord in the land of the living. Then send them a text or a note or a meal—anything to let them know God has not forgotten them.

---

## Reflection Questions

In the Hebrew language, the word for "wait" is the same as the word for "hope." Why do you think this is?

What are some of the good things the Lord revealed to you about your seasons of "inescapable hardship"?

_____

_____

_____

_____

_____

_____

_____

Why is honoring parents and covering over sin with love such a theme in the Bible?

_____

_____

_____

_____

_____

_____

_____

_____

_____

Blessed is the man who remains steadfast under trial, for when he has stood the test he will receive the crown of life, which God has promised to those who love him.

JAMES 1:12

## Group Discussion Questions

What is one inescapable hard the Lord has asked you to walk through?

How has this circumstance shaped your view of the goodness of God? (For better or worse?)

**Video Link**

What spiritual legacy has been passed down to you by your own parents?

_____

_____

_____

_____

_____

_____

_____

What is one way that you can break generational links of sin and turn the tide for your own children?

_____

_____

_____

_____

_____

_____

_____

_____

_____

_____

What is one aspect of your inescapable hard for which you can thank God?

_____

_____

_____

_____

_____

_____

_____

_____

## Prayer

*Lord, we acknowledge that every good and perfect gift comes from
You (James 1:17). Help us to shift our mindset from one of resentment
to one of looking for the good as we encounter hardship from which
we cannot escape in this lifetime. When we struggle to find joy in the
present, help us to be mindful of the joy that is coming in the future.*

# The Hard Work of Forgiveness

## IT HAS THE POWER TO CHANGE THE WAY WE MOTHER

This chapter deals with the hard work of forgiveness. The world tells us to forgive when the offending party is "truly sorry." If not, all bets are off. But Ephesians 4:32 encourages us to "be kind to one another, tenderhearted, forgiving one another, as God in Christ forgave you." Such a charge is impossible without the transforming power of the Holy Spirit at work within us. But it's so freeing when we recognize that God forgives us every time we wrong Him, and we would be hypocrites to accept that pardon without offering it to others. It doesn't mean we never have boundaries, and I recruited my mom, who has experienced more than her fair share of suffering and wrongs done in her life, to encourage us with scriptural truth in this area as well. Be encouraged: It's possible to forgive and still deal wisely with transgressors. But, oh my, is it hard!

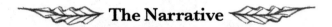 **The Narrative**

Read the examples in your book of a worldly response to hard versus a biblical response to hard. Take some time to pray about the areas in which you might be embracing a worldly "mindset of hard," and record them here. Then reflect on what those same issues might look like through a Christian perspective of biblical truth.

| THE WORLD'S RESPONSE TO HARD | A CHRISTIAN RESPONSE TO HARD |
|---|---|
|  |  |
|  |  |
|  |  |

# Action Steps

Write out, memorize, and meditate on Ephesians 4:32: "Be kind to one another, tenderhearted, forgiving one another, as God in Christ forgave you."

Ask the Lord to reveal if there is someone that you subconsciously (or consciously) believe does not deserve your forgiveness. Who did the Lord bring to mind?

Have a conversation with a trusted older woman, your husband, or your accountability partner about the unforgiveness you feel (and why you feel it) and ask them to intercede for your heart to be softened and your perspective to be shifted toward that of Christ's example of ultimate sacrifice and forgiveness. What came up during that conversation?

_____

_____

_____

_____

_____

## Reflection Questions

Why do we often tend to think of ourselves as easier to forgive or more deserving of forgiveness than those from whom we are withholding forgiveness?

_____

_____

_____

_____

_____

_____

_____

_____

What are some truths from Scripture that combat our desire to protect our right to "stay mad"?

_____

_____

_____

_____

_____

_____

_____

Is there a time in your past when you were forgiven much by someone else? If so, how has that affected your life?

_____

_____

_____

_____

_____

_____

_____

_____

_____

As the Lord has forgiven you, so you also must forgive.

COLOSSIANS 3:13

## Group Discussion Questions

Are you living in a state of unforgiveness against anyone? If so, whom and why?

Do you tend to mentally "balance the scales" of the offending party's sin against your own? If so, what does the Bible have to say about this?

**Video Link**

How can willingness to forgive (or lack thereof) affect your relationship with God and others?

_____

_____

_____

_____

_____

_____

_____

What benefits of forgiveness have you reaped from past situations?

_____

_____

_____

_____

_____

_____

_____

_____

_____

Why is forgiveness so hard?

_____

_____

_____

_____

_____

_____

_____

_____

_____

_____

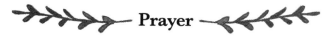 **Prayer**

*Lord, You tell us in Your Word that whoever has been forgiven
much loves much, but "whoever has been forgiven little
loves little" (Luke 7:47 NIV). Soften our hearts to recognize
just how much we have been forgiven and just how good
it is to forgive others too (even though it's so hard!).*

# Hard Is Not the Same Thing as Good

## IF IT'S NOT GOD'S WILL, IT'S JUST BAD

This chapter answers the question that might have been percolating in the back of your mind since the first chapter: So, does Abbie think all hard things are good things? No, I sure don't. And I think anyone who "embraces" hard to the point of making it an idol of sorts (or a form of punishment) is on a path to destruction and discontentment. The phrase "hard is not the same thing as bad" is merely an observation that we cannot automatically equate the two as we're so often prone to do. And yet cancer is most certainly bad. So are divorce, abuse, toxic relationships, public humiliation, adultery, and so on. The Lord can still work in our lives through them, certainly, but they are not inherently good. Our perspective is key, and biblical discernment is crucial. We must be honest and willing to assess our hard situations rightly and recognize those times we are leaning into truly harmful situations (for us and for our families). And then? We must have the humility to accept the opportunities to find better paths when the Lord leads us to them. (Because doing it just because it's hard is not the same thing as pursuing holiness.)

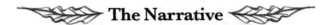 **The Narrative**

Read the examples in your book of a worldly response to hard versus a biblical response to hard. Take some time to pray about the areas in which you might be embracing a worldly "mindset of hard," and record them here. Then reflect on what those same issues might look like through a Christian perspective of biblical truth.

| THE WORLD'S RESPONSE TO HARD | A CHRISTIAN RESPONSE TO HARD |
|---|---|
| | |
| | |
| | |

## ✦ Action Steps ✦

Write down one scenario in which the hardship you're experiencing is *not* a good thing.

_____

_____

_____

_____

_____

_____

_____

Ask the Lord to show you what about this situation is outside His will for your life. What did He reveal?

_____

_____

_____

_____

_____

_____

_____

_____

_____

Commit to praying about and discussing this with your husband (or, if no husband, someone trusted and godly). What are some alternatives or solutions to the "hard-and-bad" circumstance? As the Lord reveals solutions, step forward in faith to implement them, even if they feel hard too.

## Reflection Questions

What did God reveal to me about a "hard-and-bad" situation in which I find myself?

What are some good alternatives to continuing in this situation?

How can I avoid finding myself in similar scenarios in the future?

Suffering produces endurance,
and endurance produces character,
and character produces hope.

ROMANS 5:3-4

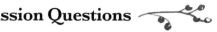

# Group Discussion Questions

What is one hard thing you're doing right now that might not be good?

Has God revealed a way forward to help you get out of this hard situation? If so, have you resisted taking the new path? Why or why not?

**Video Link**

Do you tend to cave to peer pressure when it comes to doing things just because you "should"? If so, what does this lead to?

-------------------------------------------------------------------------------

-------------------------------------------------------------------------------

-------------------------------------------------------------------------------

-------------------------------------------------------------------------------

-------------------------------------------------------------------------------

-------------------------------------------------------------------------------

-------------------------------------------------------------------------------

-------------------------------------------------------------------------------

-------------------------------------------------------------------------------

Do you know anyone else in a "hard and not good" situation? What advice would you give her?

-------------------------------------------------------------------------------

-------------------------------------------------------------------------------

-------------------------------------------------------------------------------

-------------------------------------------------------------------------------

-------------------------------------------------------------------------------

-------------------------------------------------------------------------------

-------------------------------------------------------------------------------

-------------------------------------------------------------------------------

-------------------------------------------------------------------------------

-------------------------------------------------------------------------------

What is one wise way you can gauge what kind of hard you're enduring?

---

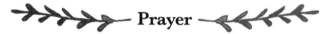

## Prayer

*Lord, we know that You give wisdom "generously to all without reproach" (James 1:5). Prod our hearts to boldly claim this truth when we find ourselves floundering in poor choices or harmful circumstances that seem beyond our control, knowing that they are never outside of Yours.*

# Finding Good Mom
# Friends Is Hard

## MAKING THE EFFORT, ESTABLISHING HEALTHY BOUNDARIES, AND LEANING INTO CONNECTIONS THAT LAST

This chapter tackles one of the most frequently addressed topics I encounter on social media: "How do I find my people?" Many of us are lonely—desperate even for the kind of connection that goes deeper than chats about the weather and grades in the bleachers at a basketball game. We are longing for the kind of friend who notices we're struggling and drops off coffee, then proceeds to help us tackle the laundry mountain on our dining room table. I'm here to tell you they exist. And yet they are often the result of years of dedicated prayer and intentional investment. I have experienced the heartache of failed relationships and toxic "friendships," and the pain of waiting and praying for years for my "tribe." It's so hard. But the hard makes the healthy relationships even sweeter when the Lord places those true sisters in Christ in our paths.

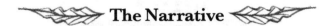 **The Narrative**

Read the examples in your book of a worldly response to hard versus a biblical response to hard. Take some time to pray about the areas in which you might be embracing a worldly "mindset of hard," and record them here. Then reflect on what those same issues might look like through a Christian perspective of biblical truth.

| THE WORLD'S RESPONSE TO HARD | A CHRISTIAN RESPONSE TO HARD |
| --- | --- |
| | |
| | |
| | |

## ❧❧❧ Action Steps ❧❧❧

Write out, memorize, and meditate on Hebrews 10:24-25: "And let us consider how to stir up one another to love and good works, not neglecting to meet together, as is the habit of some, but encouraging one another, and all the more as you see the Day drawing near."

_____

_____

_____

_____

_____

_____

Make a list of one to three friends who exemplify the friend who loves at all times (Proverbs 17:17) and then take a moment to encourage them in some way (text, voice memo, note).

1. _____

2. _____

3. _____

Write down a few names that come to mind when you think of difficult friendships. Take a moment to pray for each person by name (and don't just pray for them to "do better!").

1. _____

2. _____

3. _____

Ask the Lord to show you ways that you can be a friend to the friendless and a mentor to younger women in Christ, and record those here. We are called to serve, not simply to be served.

_____

_____

_____

_____

_____

_____

## Reflection Questions

How have good friendships made you a better Christian? How have hard ones done the same?

_____

_____

_____

_____

_____

_____

_____

_____

What are some concrete ways to invest in godly friendships in a busy season of motherhood, even if you don't yet have the friends you'd like?

Why do you think even some Christian friendships falter?

Be devoted to
one another
in love.
Honor one
another above
yourselves.

ROMANS 12:10
(NIV)

 **Group Discussion Questions**

When you think of a "best friend," what traits come to mind?

In what ways do you embody those traits? In what areas do you fall short?

**Video Link**

Whether you are in a season of abundant friendship or a period of loneliness, how is God your "ever-present help" (Psalm 46:1 NIV)?

_____

_____

_____

_____

_____

_____

_____

_____

What is something you could do to prepare yourself to be "the best friend a girl could hope for"?

_____

_____

_____

_____

_____

_____

_____

_____

_____

_____

If you have experienced a painful friendship breakup, what is one thing the Lord has taught you through the process?

_____

_____

_____

_____

_____

_____

_____

_____

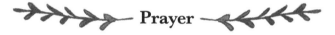 **Prayer**

*Lord, You are the Friend who never fails, never backstabs, never flakes out on us. Thank You for Your example of self-sacrificing love. Give us a desire to "cover a multitude of sin" in our own relationships, knowing that we sin, too, and that God-given friendships are one of the best ways to enjoy motherhood in community with like-minded sisters in Christ.*

# Prioritizing Marriage Is Hard

## PRACTICAL WAYS TO CHOOSE OUR SPOUSE EVEN WITH KIDS IN THE HOUSE

This chapter addresses the conundrum of prioritizing marriage while also remaining faithful in motherhood. I can't count the number of times I've been asked how in the *world*, with ten kids in the house, can Shaun and I find the energy and time for dates, sex, conversation, or even *breathing*. And while the short answer is *intentionality*, I dive deeply into some practical steps we've taken during our entire marriage to ensure that we avoid the "roommates with kids" status. The short of it: Taking proactive steps to keep our marriage strong is a lot of hard work. But it's oh-so-worth the effort!

## The Narrative

Read the examples in your book of a worldly response to hard versus a biblical response to hard. Take some time to pray about the areas in which you might be embracing a worldly "mindset of hard," and record them here. Then reflect on what those same issues might look like through a Christian perspective of biblical truth.

| THE WORLD'S RESPONSE TO HARD | A CHRISTIAN RESPONSE TO HARD |
| --- | --- |
| | |
| | |
| | |

## ⟫⟩⟩ Action Steps ⟨⟨⟨

Commit to speaking (especially) well of (and to!) your spouse for one whole week. Recruit your accountability partner to keep you on track (and do the same for her). What can you use as a reminder to help you keep this focus?

Plan a "time of focused togetherness" (a "date") within the next several weeks. Record those plans here.

Make a list of areas in which you'd like to grow in your marriage with kids in the house. Then use your date time with your spouse to brainstorm some solutions or tweaks that would make those areas better.

_____

_____

_____

_____

_____

_____

_____

## Reflection Questions

What are the hardest parts of prioritizing marriage while also being godly parents?

_____

_____

_____

_____

_____

_____

_____

_____

What are some ways that kids make marriage better?

What are some things the world says about marriage and children that directly contradict what the Bible says?

She does him good,
and not harm,
all the days of her life.
PROVERBS 31:12

**Group Discussion Questions**

What are two areas in your marriage you'd love to improve?

What have you done on a practical level to address those areas? (Yes, consistent prayer is practical!)

**Video Link**

How do you feel about the idea of a weekly date (as defined in this chapter)?

_____

_____

_____

_____

_____

_____

_____


What are the biggest parenting challenges that hinder your intimacy (physically, emotionally, spiritually) with your husband?

_____

_____

_____

_____

_____

_____

_____

_____

_____

What is holding you back from tackling those areas?

_____

_____

_____

_____

_____

_____

_____

_____

_____

_____

## Prayer

*Lord, You created marriage in response to the only thing in creation
You called "not good": Adam's being alone (Genesis 2:18). You
ordained marriage before children, and You have given it to us as a gift
but also as a picture of what the relationship between Christ and His
church should look like. Help us each prioritize marriage rightly, even
when doing so feels like too much effort in a hard season of parenting.*

# The Newborn
# Stage Is Hard

## DYING TO SELF NEVER LOOKED SO CUTE

This chapter acknowledges that, no matter how adorable, newborns can be such a challenge. The sleepless nights, the unidentifiable grunts, the diaper blowouts, the sore *everything*. What can be such a sweet time often passes in a fog of frustration and exhaustion. I see you, mama. And yet what a privilege to sustain the precious new life entrusted to us by the Father who loves us so tenderly. The newborn season is another opportunity to face our lack and take it to the foot of the cross. Be encouraged that your efforts and sacrifice are never in vain!

Read the examples in your book of a worldly response to hard versus a biblical response to hard. Take some time to pray about the areas in which you might be embracing a worldly "mindset of hard," and record them here. Then reflect on what those same issues might look like through a Christian perspective of biblical truth.

| THE WORLD'S RESPONSE TO HARD | A CHRISTIAN RESPONSE TO HARD |
| --- | --- |
| | |
| | |
| | |

## ❦ Action Steps ❦

Write out, memorize, and meditate on Ephesians 2:10: "We are his workmanship, created in Christ Jesus for good works, which God prepared beforehand, that we should walk in them."

If you're out of your first round of the newborn stage, write a letter (or at least a list) to your younger self of things you wish you'd known before becoming the mom of a tiny infant. If you're still in the newborn stage or about to be in it, ask God to send a godly woman who could share her list with you.

Sign up to take a meal to a new mom if you can. Or offer to clean her bathrooms or fold her laundry. Nothing makes a new mom feel less alone than knowing someone else has been in her shoes and "made it." Who will you reach out to?

_____

_____

_____

_____

_____

_____

## Reflection Questions

What are the best parts about the newborn stage? What are the hardest? How do both push us toward the Lord?

_____

_____

_____

_____

_____

_____

_____

_____

_____

What are some ways that our newborns' reliance on us should mirror our trust in the Lord?

How is "toxic positivity" very different from godly rejoicing (even in hard things)?

Not that I have already obtained this or am already perfect, but I press on to make it my own, because Christ Jesus has made me his own.

PHILIPPIANS 3:12

## Group Discussion Questions

Are you in the "love the newborn stage" or "not my favorite" camp? Why?

Regardless of your view, what is one thing that would have relieved some of the anxieties of this stage for you?

**Video Link**

Is there someone who comes to mind that you could provide this help to?

_____

_____

_____

_____

_____

_____

_____

_____

What are some truths we can preach to ourselves when the sleepless nights feel so long?

_____

_____

_____

_____

_____

_____

_____

_____

How does the recognition that this stage is fleeting affect your view of it?

_____

_____

_____

_____

_____

_____

_____

_____

_____

## Prayer

*Jesus, thank You for coming as a helpless infant to save us, but also, in part, to underscore what a blessing little innocent newborns are to the world. Their utter dependence is trying at times but also precious in its trust and unconditional love. Help us to see them for the treasure they are and to understand just how fleeting our time with them truly is.*

# Toddlers Are Hard

## CHOOSING TO BE THE ADULT WHEN
## WE WANT TO THROW TANTRUMS TOO

This chapter takes on the *number one* stage of motherhood I receive the most messages about: toddlers. What is going on? Why are they so undeniably adorable one moment and so blatantly unreasonable the next? Could there possibly be some design to their maddening duality? I think the answer is absolutely yes. Toddlers give us ample opportunity to confront our own desire to throw fits or succumb to our own emotions. And yet the Lord has granted us self-control and the ability to recognize their developmental limitations that keep us on the hook of being "the adult" in the scenario. Be encouraged, friends. Toddlers are a crucible absolutely worth surviving!

 **The Narrative**

Read the examples in your book of a worldly response to hard versus a biblical response to hard. Take some time to pray about the areas in which you might be embracing a worldly "mindset of hard," and record them here. Then reflect on what those same issues might look like through a Christian perspective of biblical truth.

| THE WORLD'S RESPONSE TO HARD | A CHRISTIAN RESPONSE TO HARD |
|---|---|
| | |
| | |
| | |

# Action Steps

Write out, memorize, and meditate on Galatians 6:9: "And let us not grow weary of doing good, for in due season we will reap, if we do not give up."

Unfollow accounts that mock and degrade toddlers for their frustrating behaviors. What types of accounts did you unfollow?

Make yourself sticky notes to post around the house (or car) reminding you of the things you love most about the awesome-but-hard little person you are mothering. How has this practice helped your perspective?

_____

_____

_____

_____

_____

## Reflection Questions

What are three ways toddlers are awesome?

1. _____

2. _____

3. _____

What are three ways toddlers are hard?

1. _____

2. _____

3. _____

How can God use both to reveal His goodness to us?

Why do some mothers cling so tightly to their right to despise the toddler phase?

How has the Bible called us to view young children?

_____

_____

_____

_____

_____

_____

_____

_____

## Group Discussion Questions

What messages does "the world" send us about toddlers?

_____

_____

_____

_____

_____

_____

_____

_____

_____

_____

In what ways are they right? And wrong?

What are your favorite things about this phase? Least favorite?

**Video Link**

I will ... boast all
the more ... gladly
of my ... weaknesses,
so that the ... power of
Christ may ... rest upon me.

2 CORINTHIANS 12:9

What does the Bible tell us about little children?

How does our modeling calm and self-control to our toddlers prepare them for phases to come?

## Prayer

*Lord, may Your gracious response of "let the little children come to me and do not hinder them, for to such belongs the kingdom of heaven" (Matthew 19:14) be our guide for how we treat our own toddlers. Give us Your supernatural grace to handle frustrating experiences with wisdom and patience, knowing that You extend those same gifts to us daily.*

# Connecting with Teenagers Is Hard

## THE ART OF CHOOSING OUR YESES LAVISHLY AND OUR NOES WISELY

This chapter addresses the stage that strikes the most fear into every parent's heart: teens. Although I understand the logic behind the dread associated with this phase, I am here to tell you that it doesn't have to be all sullen standoffs and sneaking out. In fact, it can be neither of those, depending on the teen, and something else entirely—either challenging or delightful. The point is that we refuse to pigeonhole an entire age category into something to be feared and avoided. Instead, we invest with dogged intentionality and fearless love. As a mama to three teens (and two more in the wings!), I can honestly say that I have scratched my head at the complexity of their emotions and thrown my hands in the air with joy at the beauty of their connection. In my experience, while certain aspects of parenting teens have been challenges, the vast majority of my experiences have been overwhelmingly positive. Be encouraged: Lovingly and wisely holding the line, even as they begin to spread their wings, is your job, and the Lord has equipped you to do it well.

## The Narrative

Read the examples in your book of a worldly response to hard versus a biblical response to hard. Take some time to pray about the areas in which you might be embracing a worldly "mindset of hard," and record them here. Then reflect on what those same issues might look like through a Christian perspective of biblical truth.

| THE WORLD'S RESPONSE TO HARD | A CHRISTIAN RESPONSE TO HARD |
|---|---|
| | |
| | |
| | |

## Action Steps

Write out, memorize, and meditate on Romans 13:8: "Owe no one anything, except to love each other, for the one who loves another has fulfilled the law."

_____

_____

_____

Make a list of three things your teenager(s) love(s) to do. Put them on your calendar this week.

1. _____

2. _____

3. _____

Ask your accountability partner to pray for your resolve to preach truth to your teens, a genuine desire to show love to your teens, and perseverance to be a consistent Christlike model for your teens. Record here the prayer requests she has for you.

_____

_____

_____

_____

_____

_____

_____

A fool vents
all his anger,
but a wise man
holds it
back.

PROVERBS 29:11
(BSB)

# Reflection Questions

How does the world's view of "teenagerdom" differ from the Bible's exhortations to young adults (especially in Proverbs)?

What are three ways that teenagers are awesome? Three ways they're hard? How can the Lord use both for good in our lives?

How would viewing my teen as a future peer (and hopefully sister or brother in Christ)—and taking responsibility for the influence I have on them—change my treatment of them or attitude toward them now?

_____

_____

_____

_____

_____

_____

## Group Discussion Questions

If you are not already a mom of teens, what emotions does the prospect of parenting them bring up?

_____

_____

_____

_____

_____

_____

_____

_____

_____

_____

What influences (positive and negative) contribute to these emotions?

What are some wise boundaries you can plan for yourself (and stick to) in your kids' teen years?

**Video Link**

Who is someone wise you admire from whom you could seek godly counsel about the teen years?

_____

_____

_____

_____

_____

_____

_____

What is something joyful in parenting you remember, either from being a teen whose parent did well or from being a mom to a teen?

_____

_____

_____

_____

_____

_____

_____

_____

_____

 **Prayer**

*Lord, You love our teens, even when we struggle to like them
sometimes. You encourage us not to look down on young men
and women simply because they are young (1 Timothy 4:12), and
You exhort us to be patient with everyone, "bearing with one
another in love" (Ephesians 4:2). Help us to see our teens with
Your eyes and invest in them with care and intentionality.*

# Motherhood Is Hard

## REJECTING A MARTYR COMPLEX
## TO CHOOSE TRUE JOY

This chapter wraps up our time together with the simple truth that "motherhood is hard." But it also acknowledges that if we dwell only there, we will miss out on so many rich truths and experiences with which motherhood blesses us. Yes, it will be a struggle to choose to see the good in the midst of a culture clamoring to assure us that the effort to mother consistently and well simply requires too much of us. That it drains us. That we are "sucked dry" by its demands. But the Bible is crystal clear that in laying down our lives to invest in the eternal souls that have been entrusted to us, we are sharing, in some small part, in the sufferings of Christ—and in the glory of His sacrifice as well. We are partnering with Jesus in taking up our crosses daily to serve and love and protect. What a privilege! No motherhood hardship is wasted when we do it for the Lord.

## ~~≫≫≫~~ The Narrative ~~≪≪≪~~

Read the examples in your book of a worldly response to hard versus a biblical response to hard. Take some time to pray about the areas in which you might be embracing a worldly "mindset of hard," and record them here. Then reflect on what those same issues might look like through a Christian perspective of biblical truth.

| THE WORLD'S RESPONSE TO HARD | A CHRISTIAN RESPONSE TO HARD |
| --- | --- |
| | |
| | |
| | |

## Action Steps

Write out, memorize, and meditate on Philippians 3:14: "Press on toward the goal for the prize of the upward call of God in Christ Jesus."

---

---

---

---

---

---

---

Write out a "Mama Manifesto"—a statement of truth about what kind of mother you are (or desire to be) and why. Take your time on this. You want it to be something you can prayerfully return to on hard mothering days to remind you why the effort and sacrifice are all worth it.

---

---

---

---

---

---

---

---

Make a list of three things that you have "found" in "losing yourself" to motherhood.

1. _____

_____

2. _____

_____

3. _____

_____

## Reflection Questions

What hard-but-good insight(s) would you add to the list that I shared from my readers?

_____

_____

_____

_____

_____

_____

_____

_____

_____

Why is an attitude of martyrdom in motherhood so antithetical to what Scripture teaches us about dying to self?

_____

_____

_____

_____

_____

_____

_____

_____

What are three specific ways that God is calling you "toward the goal for the prize of the upward call of God"?

_____

_____

_____

_____

_____

_____

_____

_____

_____

_____

# Group Discussion Questions

Before you became a mama, what did you expect your role to look like?

How did the reality of motherhood compare with your expectations?

What messages do you hear the loudest about the hard aspects of motherhood from social media, books, and culture at large?

If negative, how are these messages shortsighted when compared with the eternal perspective of Scripture?

**Video Link**

PRESS ON TOWARD THE GOAL FOR THE PRIZE OF THE UPWARD CALL OF GOD IN CHRIST JESUS.

PHILIPPIANS 3:14

What is the best hard thing you have encountered in motherhood? Why?

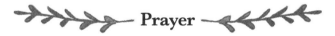 **Prayer**

*Lord, it is a privilege and a blessing to lose ourselves to be found in You. Thank You for the opportunity each day to share in Your sufferings and joys through the calling of motherhood. Clarify our vision to see the truth of what an honor it is to be called "Mama."*

# Conclusion

Since the Lord gave me the phrase "hard is not the same thing as bad" (on a walk with my best friend almost ten years ago), it is the single thing I've shared for which I've received the most feedback! I've fielded hundreds of messages from women around the world who have assured me that these eight little words have been the fuel that has gotten them through toddler meltdowns and marriage struggles, through parental sickness and personal loss. And I'm so grateful (and a bit blown away). I never imagined the impact it could have, but I do know, firsthand, that God can use even the simplest truths to transform our hearts and minds.

If you've been doing this study on your own and it has been beneficial to you, I would encourage you to take chapter 10 to heart and use it as a jumping-off point to establish connections with other moms who are looking to buck a worldly view of hard. As you pray for, encourage, exhort, and hold each other accountable through a group study of *Hard Is Not the Same Thing as Bad*, your group will be able to very practically bear one another's burdens and lessen the difficulty of so many aspects of mother-hood that were never meant to be confronted in isolation.

I pray, if you choose a group study, the Lord blesses your time richly with both encouragement and conviction!

**Video Link**

# Organizing a Six- or Eight-Week Study

B elow, you'll find suggestions for how to break the book's chapters up for a six- or eight-week study. Of course, you can do what works best for the group.

### Six-week study

Week 1—intro, chapters 1 and 2
Week 2—3, 4, 5
Week 3—6, 7, 8
Week 4—9, 10, 11
Week 5—12, 13, 14
Week 6—15

### Eight-week study

Week 1—intro, chapters 1 and 2
Week 2—3, 4
Week 3—5, 6
Week 4—7, 8
Week 5—9, 10
Week 6—11, 12
Week 7—13, 14
Week 8—15

# Group Study Guidelines
# for Busy Mamas

## PLAN BEFOREHAND

Before you announce the study and start inviting other mamas to join you, you'll want to determine some basic parameters. This ensures that you will be able to fulfill your role as leader without feeling frazzled in the process.

Here are some items you will want to decide prior to announcing the study:

1. **Where are we meeting?** Whether at your church, your home, a local coffee shop, or a restaurant, it is key to select a location that's convenient for you and offers enough room for the group you invite. If you plan to meet in a public area, one factor to consider is privacy. Will mamas be hesitant to share in a place their friends and neighbors frequent? This may not be an issue, but it's something to think about.

   A virtual study is also a great option (I've seen huge success with these!), but keep in mind the potential hiccups that come with online meetings—tech issues, background noise, not to mention the disconnect that comes with not being physically present as a group. Don't underestimate the value of a hug from another mama who understands what you're going through.

2. **When will we be meeting?** This is a huge issue for mamas. The main thing to ensure is that the time you choose works for you. If you're struggling to keep the time you committed to, leading the group will become an unwelcome chore, or worse yet, you'll want to quit it altogether. No time you choose will be convenient for all the mamas you invite, so don't feel guilty if one or two bow out because it doesn't fit their schedule.

   Knowing if most of the mamas in your group work or are stay-at-home or homeschool moms might make a difference, but don't assume just because a mama stays at home and her children are at school that she can drop everything and attend a midday study. Determine the best time for you and your family, and trust that God will bring the mamas to the study who need to hear the book's message. No regrets.

3. **Who will be in my group?** Determining what mamas you'll recruit to join your study might make a big difference in deciding the other details. Will you be inviting moms from your church? Your neighborhood? Your network of friends? If from church, consider putting a cap on the number of people who can sign up for the study, or make sure you have a meeting space that can accommodate a bigger group.

4. **Will childcare be available?** Because this is a book for mamas, you can't plan a study without considering the kiddos! Though it's perfectly fine to meet somewhere and not bring the children (especially if you're meeting at a coffee shop or restaurant), you will get a better turnout (and be more inclusive of single mamas) if members know they can bring their kiddos, and someone trustworthy is there to watch them. If you're meeting at church, is there a church member or youth group worker available to help?

If at home, is there a responsible older sibling looking to make a few extra bucks? Also, don't rule out dads. Many hubbies would be thrilled to help with this! Last, consider "embracing the chaos" and meeting in a kid-friendly place where the little ones can roam close by and play while you meet and talk. Moms are fantastic multitaskers, and many successful *Hard Is Not the Same Thing as Bad* studies (with kids!) have already taken place at a local park or play place, or even in someone's backyard.

5. **How long will the study last? And how long will we meet each week?** Again, this might come down to what works best for you. Ideally, you could read a chapter per week and give yourself plenty of time to digest the content, but that's not going to be possible for most groups, which is why I've included plans for six- and eight-week studies.

   If you choose a longer time, be prepared to accept that mamas might drop out as the study goes on. Generally, you will get more commitments to a shorter time frame. Reading several chapters a week might sound daunting to some mamas, but the good news is the chapters are short and easy reads.

   Encourage your members to dig in for the short term so they can experience the benefits in the long term!

   As for the duration of each meeting, this is entirely up to you, but anything longer than an hour per week might be a hindrance to some moms.

## READ THE BOOK FIRST

Though reading it first isn't mandatory to lead the group, you will feel more prepared if you read the book prior to starting the study. This will make it easier for you to facilitate group discussions and answer questions from your fellow mamas. If you're stepping up to lead this group, chances are you've already read the book. Fist bump, mama!

## BE TRANSPARENT

If you have read the book, you know that I'm not shy about sharing my own frustrations and foibles as a mama. I get regular emails from readers who were encouraged by what I share, but the material will really start to sink in if mamas are willing to discuss with the group their own personal trials and triumphs. This might require you to take the lead to help create a space where mamas feel comfortable to share. The more your group is transparent about their journeys as mamas, the more you will get out of your study time. One point to consider here is confidentiality. Establishing an up-front rule that whatever is shared in the group stays only in the group will encourage more open discussions. It also helps the group stay accountable to one another and avoid the temptation of gossiping.

## PRAY, PRAY, PRAY

Though this suggestion might seem obvious, it bears mentioning. Pray over your group. Pray to start and end each meeting. Leave time for prayer requests. Remember that one of the main points of the book is to apply biblical wisdom to raising our children. This can't be done without prayer…and lots of it. Ask God to reveal what He wants you to learn each week and how you can pray for others in the group.

# More Biblical Wisdom
# for Mamas Like You

See how God can use the everyday trials of child raising to radically transform how you view hardship and grow you to become more like Jesus.

Humbly and gracefully rise to the high calling of motherhood without settling for mediocrity or losing your mind in the process.

## ABOUT ABBIE

**Abbie Halberstadt** is a happy wife and mama of ten children, including two sets of identical twins. She's also a homeschool educator, fitness instructor, business owner, speaker, and writer. Through her blog and social media posts, she encourages women to dig deep to meet the challenges of everyday life. She, her husband, Shaun, and their children live in the Piney Woods of East Texas.

MIsForMama.net